A HISTORY OF BRITAIN

PAPERBIRD

Acknowledgments:

The publishers would like to acknowledge the use of additional illustrative material as follows: Aerofilms, page 47; Anglo-Saxon Trust, cover and page 9; Ashmolean Museum, cover and page 20; AA Photolibrary, page 12 (bottom); Crown copyright, page 38; Crown copyright, Public Record Office, page 43; BBC Hulton Picture Library, page 32 (top); British Library, pages 31 (top right), 46; English Heritage, page 37; Hedingham Castle, page 39; A F Kersting, page 13; Lloyd and Jennifer Laing, page 31 (top left); Mary Evans Picture Library, page 21; Mats Wibe Lund, page 16; Michael Holford, cover and pages 32-33; National Museum of Ireland, Dublin, page 25; Royal Commission on Ancient Monuments, Scotland, page 12 (top); The Master and Fellows of Corpus Christi College, Cambridge, page 28, Trustees of the British Museum, cover and pages 7, 26, 50, 51; Werner Forman Archive, page 15 (bottom left); WFA/National Museum, Copenhagen, page 44; WFA/Statens Historiska Museum, Stockholm, pages 15 (bottom right), 17; Woodmansterne Picture Library, page 49. John Dillow, illustrations on pages 4-5, 52-53 and hand lettering on pages 20 and 43; Anne Matthews, illustration on page 18 (bottom left).

Designed by Gavin Young.

British Library Cataloguing in Publication Data

Wood, Tim
    The Saxons and the Normans.
    1. England, to 1066   2. England, 1066-1154
    I. Title   II. Page, Phil   III. Series
    942.01
    ISBN 1-85543-007-X

Published by Ladybird Books Ltd Loughborough Leicestershire UK
Ladybird Books Inc Auburn Maine 04210 USA
Paperbird is an imprint of Ladybird Books Ltd
© LADYBIRD BOOKS LTD MCMLXXXIX

Printed in England

Contents

Interesting places to visit – page 56

The
Saxons
and the
Normans

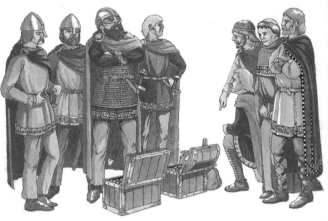

by TIM WOOD

illustrations by PHIL PAGE

Series Consultants: School of History
University of Bristol

Paperbird

nglo-Saxons, Vikings and Normans

This book covers a period of nearly nine hundred years, from the end of Roman rule to 1272.

During this time Britain was invaded by many different groups of people. Each group brought its own customs and traditions, which soon replaced the old Roman way of life. Gradually the invaders settled and became Britons themselves.

Anglo-Saxons to Normans time chart

Date	Kings and people	What happened
400		Roman legions leave Britain. Saxon raids. St Patrick goes to Ireland
500	St Columba St Augustine	Christian missionaries come to Britain
600		The Seven Kingdoms. Sutton Hoo ship burial (625). Spread of Christianity. Synod of Whitby (664)
700	Offa, King of Mercia 758-796	Viking raids begin
800	Alfred 871-899 Guthrum, Danish leader, defeated by Alfred in 878	The Vikings settle in England. Danes defeated. Peace of Wedmore. Danes conquer Normandy
900	Edward the Elder 899-924	Conquest of the Danelaw
	Athelstan 924-939	Southern Scotland conquered
	Edmund, Eadred, Eadwig 939-959 Eric Bloodaxe, last Viking King of York	Defeat of Danes raiding from Ireland. Northumbria conquered
	Edgar 959-975 St Dunstan, Archbishop of Canterbury	The first coronation

Date	Kings and people	What happened
1000	Ethelred the 'ill-advised' 978-1015	Danish raids begin again. Danegeld
	Edmund 'Ironside' 1015 Sweyn Forkbeard Cnut 1016-1035	Peace between the English and the Danes
	Edward the Confessor 1042-1066 Tostig Harald of Norway	Westminster Abbey begun. Battle of Stamford Bridge
	Harold January to October, 1066	Appearance of Halley's comet. Battle of Hastings.
	William I 1066-1087 Hereward the Wake opposes William in the fen country	*Bayeux Tapestry* Many castles built. *Domesday Book* (1086)
	William II 1087-1100	Jerusalem captured by Turks. First Crusade (1096), led by Peter the hermit
1100	Henry I 1100-1135	Strong rule. Wreck of the White Ship (Henry's son, William, drowned)
	Stephen 1135-1154	Stephen and his cousin, Matilda, fight for control of the throne and the country. Barons start building strong castles. Second Crusade: failed to capture Damascus
1150	**THE PLANTAGENETS** Henry II 1154-1189 Eleanor of Aquitaine marries Henry II. Thomas Becket, Archbishop of Canterbury	New French lands added to possessions in England. New law courts
	Richard I 1189-1199 Saladin, Sultan of Egypt	Third Crusade, attended by Richard I. Acre captured. Battle of Arsouf. Richard captured in Austria
1200	John 1199-1216	War with France. Loss of Normandy. Magna Carta (1215). War with the Barons
	Henry III 1216-1272 Simon de Montfort	The Oxford Parliament

Anglo-Saxon settlers

In 383, over fifteen hundred years ago, the Roman legions gradually began to leave Britain to fight in Gaul (France) against the Barbarian tribes who were invading the Roman Empire. By 407, there were not enough Roman soldiers left to defend Britain from the Picts and Scots, fierce raiders from the North.

There were four main groups of German settlers – Angles, Saxons, Frisians and Jutes.

The British chiefs asked Anglo-Saxon soldiers to come from Germany to fight for them. In return for this help, the Anglo-Saxons were given land. Some already lived in Britain and had fought in the Roman army.

The Anglo-Saxons were strong soldiers. They defeated the Picts and Scots and, when the Britons asked them to leave, they refused to go. As time passed more and more Anglo-Saxons arrived, wanting land and attacking the Britons. Soon they began to settle in Britain.

A restored shield, found in the Anglo-Saxon ship buried at Sutton Hoo, Suffolk. It belonged to an East Anglian chief, perhaps a king

The Anglo-Saxons rowed across the North Sea in small boats. They fought the Britons and often won. Legend tells of a great British war leader who lived at this time and fought against the invaders. His name was Arthur

Anglo-Saxon villages

The Anglo-Saxon settlers rowed up the rivers looking for good places to build their villages. The best sites were easy to defend and had a good supply of water and wood.

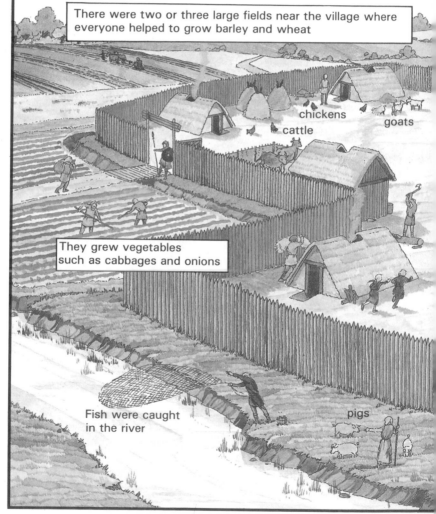

There were two or three large fields near the village where everyone helped to grow barley and wheat

chickens

goats

cattle

They grew vegetables such as cabbages and onions

Fish were caught in the river

pigs

This *replica* Anglo-Saxon house from the West Stow village, was built with the same kinds of tools and materials used by the Saxons

thatch made from reeds or straw

The chief and the richer villagers lived in large houses

loom for weaving cloth

wall made from split tree trunks

quern for grinding corn into flour

Poorer people lived in small houses built over pits in the ground. Some had wooden floorboards to keep the floor dry

The Anglo-Saxon kingdoms

For about one hundred and fifty years the Britons fought the Anglo-Saxons, but by the year 600 the Britons had either been forced to flee to Wales and the West Country or had become slaves.

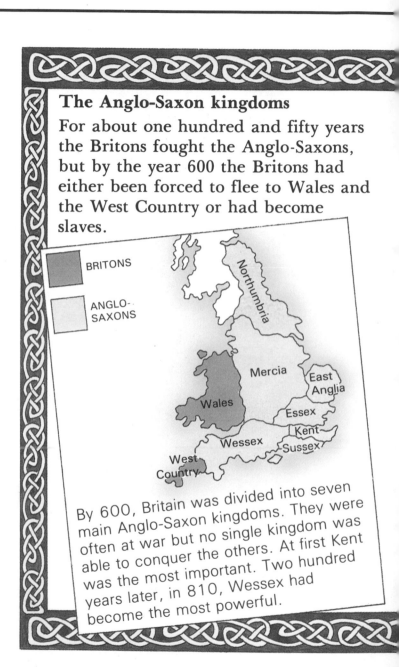

BRITONS

ANGLO-SAXONS

Northumbria

Mercia

East Anglia

Wales

Essex

Kent

Wessex

Sussex

West Country

By 600, Britain was divided into seven main Anglo-Saxon kingdoms. They were often at war but no single kingdom was able to conquer the others. At first Kent was the most important. Two hundred years later, in 810, Wessex had become the most powerful.

How a kingdom was organised

The KING gave gifts of weapons and land to his people. In return they fought for him. He was advised by a group of councillors called the Witan

The THANES were the nobles. They owned a lot of land and were expected to fight for the king. Some were made *ealdormen* and acted as judges and rulers in their areas

The CHURLS were free peasants who owned some land. They paid taxes and fought for their thane. They had to take part in village meetings called folk moots, which were held whenever there were arguments about land

SLAVES could be bought, sold or given away. A slave could be worth as much as eight oxen. Many were British prisoners taken in battle, while others were born into slavery. Later Alfred, King of Wessex, passed laws allowing slaves to sell things they had made and to own some property

Christianity

The Anglo-Saxons were *pagans*, who did not believe in the Christian God. There were still groups of Christians, some of whom were descended from the Roman Britons (*Celts*), living in parts of Ireland and Wales. Gradually these Celtic Christians returned to England and Scotland, and began to *convert* the Picts, Scots and Anglo-Saxons.

St Columba's church on Iona. He converted the northern Picts and brought Christianity to Scotland in 563

Iona

St Patrick took Christianity to Ireland in 432

a Celtic cross

The Synod of Whitby, 664

Gradually most of Britain became Christian. The Celtic Christians followed St Columba. The southern Christians followed St Augustine, from Rome. They argued about many things. A *synod*, held in Whitby, Yorkshire, settled the arguments and the two groups of Christians in time united in the Roman Catholic Church.

Aidan, a monk from Iona, set up a monastery at Lindisfarne in 634

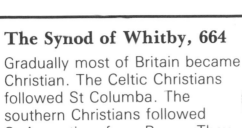

Lindisfarne

Whitby

Lindisfarne today. At high tide it is an island

Key
- ■ Celtic Christians
- □ Roman Christians

St Augustine was sent by Pope Gregory from Rome in 597. He converted Ethelbert, the Saxon king of Kent

Canterbury

Viking raiders

In 789, more than three hundred years after the Anglo-Saxons had begun to settle in Britain, the first *Viking* raiders landed near Weymouth, Dorset. They did little damage but a few years later more Vikings returned. They attacked the monasteries at Lindisfarne and Jarrow, killing monks, stealing treasure from churches and capturing slaves.

The Vikings came from Norway, Sweden and Denmark. The winters there were long and cold, and the soil was poor. Britain was a rich prize for them.

A Viking longship carried about eighty men who rowed and sailed the ship and then fought on land using swords and battle axes. The ships were strong enough to sail on rough seas and shallow enough to sail up rivers, deep into Britain.

Soon Viking raids were happening almost every year. In 851, a huge fleet of over three hundred and fifty Viking ships attacked the south of England and then, instead of sailing home across the North Sea, for the first time the raiders spent the winter in Kent.

a Swedish helmet similar to the type used by the Vikings

the hilt of a Viking sword, from Sweden

Viking settlers

About eighty years after their first attack, the Vikings formed a 'Great Army' to conquer Britain and seven years later only the kingdom of Wessex remained free of them.

Many Vikings settled in lonely parts of Britain, such as the Shetland Islands. These replica Viking houses in Iceland show what the Shetland houses may have looked like. The Viking settlers lived by farming, fishing and trading

When the Vikings took the Anglo-Saxon Kingdom of Northumbria they made Jorvik (York) its Viking capital.

Jorvik became an important Viking trading centre, where merchants visited from all over the world. It was a rich town with craftsmen producing beautiful jewellery as well as objects made from wood and bone. Cloth and wheat were traded for wine and silk from abroad.

Viking jewellery

Jorvik houses were made mainly of wood with thatched roofs. They were crammed close together and the streets were dirty and smelly

17

Alfred the Great

In 871, Alfred became King of Wessex. The Vikings soon attacked his kingdom, but Alfred managed to escape and hid in the Athelney marshes in Somerset. He gathered an army and defeated the Viking King, Guthrum, at the battle of Edington, near Chippenham. The Vikings surrendered.

WALES

DANELAW

MERCIA

WESSEX

King Alfred and the Vikings made a treaty. The Vikings were to live in an area called the Danelaw, where they were allowed to follow Viking customs and obey the 'Danes' law'.

A statue of Alfred was put up in Winchester, Alfred's capital, in 1901

Alfred did not trust the Danes. He ordered ships and fortified towns called *burhs* to be built to protect England from possible Viking attack.

His new army called the *fyrd* was divided into two halves. One half was ready to fight at any time, while the other half farmed the land. Then, after a time, the two swapped over.

The *Anglo-Saxon Chronicle*

Alfred wanted to educate his people. He invited teachers to come from Europe and ordered monks to write books in Anglo-Saxon. One book was an important history of Britain called the *Anglo-Saxon Chronicle*, which told the story of Britain from the birth of Christ. Monks also translated the Bible into Anglo-Saxon.

This is the entry in the *Chronicle* for the year 900. Alfred died in 899 according to the modern calendar, not in use when the *Chronicle* was written.

.... in this year Alfred the son of Aethelwulf died, six days before All Saints' day. He was king over the whole English people except for that part which was under Danish rule, and he had held the kingdom for one and half years less than thirty; and then his son Edward succeeded to the kingdom.

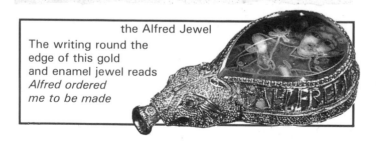

the Alfred Jewel

The writing round the edge of this gold and enamel jewel reads *Alfred ordered me to be made*

One of Alfred's Schools

The sons of nobles and boys who were to become priests were taught to read and write. They also learned geography, Latin and history

a page from the
Anglo-Saxon Chronicle

Alfred's laws

When Alfred became King of Wessex, he found that different laws were used in different parts of his kingdom. He introduced his own laws from old Saxon customs, and many good laws from other kingdoms.

People who were accused of crimes had to appear in front of the village moot. If they did not appear for their trial they were declared outlaws and could be killed by anyone.

Those who admitted their crime had to pay a fine to anyone they had harmed. In the case of murder the fine was called *wergild*. The size of the wergild depended on the importance of the injured person. The more important the victim, the higher the wergild.

Trial by ordeal

If accused people could not find enough oath-helpers (people who would swear they were innocent), they were tried by 'ordeal'. The Anglo-Saxons believed that God would judge whether the person were guilty or not.

The accused person either picked a stone out of a pan of boiling water or carried a bar of red-hot iron for several paces. If the scalded or burned hand had begun to heal after three days, the person was innocent. If not, he or she was guilty.

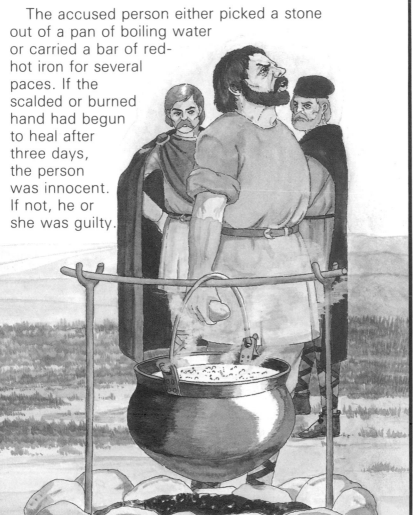

Sports and pastimes

For nearly one hundred years after Alfred's death in 899, the Anglo-Saxons and the Danes lived in their separate kingdoms. There were problems, quarrels and wars but during times of peace both groups enjoyed themselves.

Rich Anglo-Saxons liked riding and hunting

Children played games such as wrestling and sword fighting, which trained them for war

The Danes enjoyed sports like weightlifting using heavy boulders, which showed off their strength, but they also liked gentler pastimes. We know that they played board games because some have been found in graves, although the rules are not known.

The Danes raised fierce, wild stallions which were bred for fighting

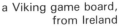

a Viking game board, from Ireland

Feasting

The Anglo-Saxons and the Vikings loved feasting. The guests ate large amounts of roast and boiled meat with bread, peas and cabbage. This food was washed down with vast quantities of beer, wine and *mead*. There was much laughter and boasting and, no doubt, some quarrelling and fighting as well.

Slaves served the food

lyre

Anglo-Saxon drinking horns, found at Sutton Hoo. Horns like these were also used by the Vikings. They enjoyed drinking competitions.

Viking poets recited poems called sagas, which told of the adventures and brave deeds of heroes and gods.

Everyone ate with their fingers

England after Alfred

Within thirty years of Alfred's death, England had become a united country. There were three kings who helped to make the peace. Alfred's son, Edward, and grandson, Athelstan, conquered the Danelaw. A few years later, Viking raids from Ireland and Norway were defeated, and Athelstan made peace with the Welsh and the Northumbrians.

An Anglo-Saxon picture of King Athelstan, who ruled from 924 to 939. He conquered Northumbria and by the end of his reign was called 'King of the Anglo-Saxons'

King Edgar encouraged the building of many new monasteries and, at the end of his reign in 975, most of England was peaceful and prosperous.

Some Anglo-Saxon histories record that in 975, eight lesser kings from the north and Scotland rowed King Edgar's boat on the river Dee. There, they swore loyalty to Edgar and, although the story may not be true, it shows how powerful the English King had become by this time.

Danegeld

In 980, Danish raids on England began again. The King, Ethelred, was not able to defeat the invaders so he paid them large amounts of silver and gold to go. This money (called *Danegeld*) simply made the Danes eager for more and they returned in greater numbers.

Within forty years, they had conquered the Anglo-Saxons and King Sweyn of Denmark became the first Danish King of England.

Ethelred raised the Danegeld through taxes. On one occasion he paid £16,000 in silver to the Danes

An Anglo-Saxon coin. Danegeld was paid in money like this. Many payments were made, one of the largest being 82,500 pounds in weight of silver and gold demanded by King Cnut to pay his army.

A picture of Cnut, Sweyn's son, who became King of England after his father. In spite of the fears of the Anglo-Saxons, he was a very fair king. His two sons followed him on the throne. Then, when the second son died, Ethelred's son, Edward, returned from France to become King of England.

Struggle for the throne

Edward the Confessor

Edward was not a strong king. He rebuilt Westminster Abbey and was later known as 'the confessor', which means 'strong believer in Christianity'. Edward died without a son to follow him. Three men each claimed the right to be the next king.

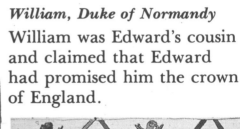

William, Duke of Normandy

William was Edward's cousin and claimed that Edward had promised him the crown of England.

Harald Hardrada, King of Norway

Harald Hardrada was a Viking who wanted to join England to his kingdoms in Norway and Sweden. He was helped by Tostig, ex-Earl of Northumbria, the treacherous brother of Harold of Wessex.

Harold, Earl of Wessex

Harold was the most powerful Anglo-Saxon earl in England. In 1064, he fought for William and swore to support the Duke of Normandy's claim to the English throne. Harold said later that, just before Edward had died, the old King had promised *him* the crown of England.

◀ This scene from the *Bayeux Tapestry* shows Harold of Wessex swearing a holy oath to support William

hAROLD AND WILLIAM

1. HAROLD OF WESSEX WAS CROWNED BY EALDRED, ARCHBISHOP OF YORK, IN JANUARY 1066

2. WILLIAM, FEELING CHEATED, GATHERED AN ARMY TO INVADE ENGLAND

3. THE SHIPS WERE DELAYED BY BAD WEATHER

4. HARALD, KING OF NORWAY, INVADED NORTHERN ENGLAND IN SEPTEMBER

5 HAROLD MARCHED NORTH AND DEFEATED HARALD AT THE BATTLE OF STAMFORD BRIDGE

6 A FEW DAYS LATER WILLIAM'S FLEET LANDED NEAR HASTINGS. HE WAITED FOR HAROLD

7 HAROLD MARCHED SOUTH, NOT WAITING TO GATHER A LARGER ARMY

8 ON 13TH OCTOBER, HAROLD AND HIS SAXON ARMY REACHED HASTINGS...

The Battle of Hastings

The battle began at nine o'clock in the morning on 14th October 1066. The English locked their shields together to make a wall and defended the top of a hill with axes and swords.

The Normans, most of whom were trained knights on horses, charged up the hill all morning but could not break through the shield wall. But many of the English left the safety of the shield wall to chase the Norman knights and were killed. Gradually the English army began to break up.

Late in the afternoon, while the Norman archers fired high in the air, raining arrows down on the English, the Norman knights charged again. This time they broke through the weakened shield wall. Harold was killed and the rest of his army fled.

William marched to London, burning and destroying buildings and farmland as he went. The city, with no king and no army to defend it, surrendered.

Battle Abbey was built on the site of the battle

Norman castles

William was crowned King of England on Christmas Day 1066, and for the next one hundred years England was ruled by the Normans.

There were over two million Anglo-Saxons in England and only ten thousand Norman knights. To make it easier to control the people, William and his *barons* built castles all over the country.

The bailey – a courtyard where animals and villagers from the surrounding land could stay during an attack

stables and huts

The White Tower at the Tower of London, built by William I about 1078

The first castles, which were wooden, were built very quickly and often the English were forced to do the work. Later castles, like this one at Berkhamsted, which was finished one hundred years after the Battle of Hastings, were built of stone.

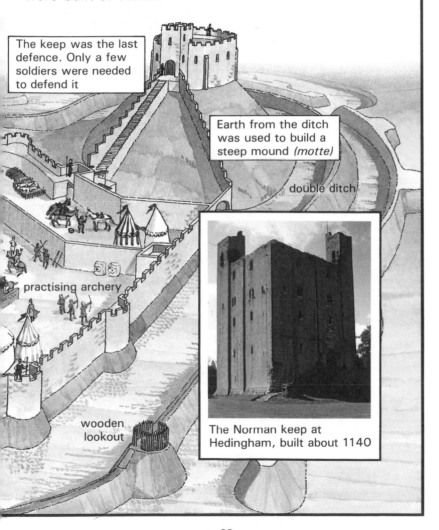

The keep was the last defence. Only a few soldiers were needed to defend it

Earth from the ditch was used to build a steep mound *(motte)*

double ditch

practising archery

wooden lookout

The Norman keep at Hedingham, built about 1140

King and tenants

William owned the whole of England, with all its land and people. He had to make sure that the Normans would always help one another and support him. William gave his supporters land on condition that they fought for him. Historians call this *feudalism*.

Almost half the land in England was given to about two hundred tenants-in-chief, who were mostly Norman.

The tenants-in-chief (church leaders and barons) held the land only as long as they swore to be loyal to the King. The barons paid rent by providing soldiers and paying taxes to the King. They divided their land into smaller areas, called *fees (fiefs)*, and allowed *tenants* (often knights) to live on them

A tenant held the land only as long as he swore to be loyal to his baron. Tenants paid rent by providing soldiers and paying taxes to the barons. In turn, tenants allowed the peasants to work on their land

Peasants were allowed to work on the land provided they also worked for the tenants and paid them taxes. A peasant could not leave the land unless the tenant allowed him to do so

How
fcudalism
worked

The *Domesday Book*

William needed to know more about England. He wanted to find out how much the land was worth so that he could work out what taxes everyone should pay. He also wanted to make sure that none of his followers had taken land which did not belong to them.

William sent teams of officials, called commissioners, to every corner of the country to find out about his new kingdom. They asked questions in every village.

The commissioners and their clerks wrote down the answers, which were later put into two volumes called the *Domesday Book*. 'Domesday' means 'The Day of Judgement'.

Here are some of the questions which were asked for the *Domesday Book*.

Who holds the land?
How many ploughs are there?
How much land is good for growing crops?
How much is just wasteland?
How much is the land worth?

the *Domesday Book*

What people wore

Fashions changed greatly during the time of the Anglo-Saxons, the Vikings and the Normans. Most clothes were made of wool or linen, dyed with vegetable dyes.

Viking warrior

tunic

trousers

Viking woman

Married women wore white headscarves

'tortoise' brooches

Saxon thane

Leather cross-garters kept the hose, or stockings, in place

Viking 'tortoise' brooches from Denmark – so called because of their shape

Men's cloaks were usually fastened on the right shoulder to leave the sword arm free. When fighting, knights wore armour, made of iron rings sewn onto a leather coat called a hauberk.

Norman knight

hauberk – slit for horseriding

kite-shaped shield

spurs

chausses

Norman baron

hair shaved at the back

over tunic

under tunic

Norman lady

leather shoes

over tunic – laced at the sides

outer tunic

inner tunic

Saxon woman

The Crusades

William's descendants, especially Henry II, the first *Plantagenet* king, gained a huge empire in France. However Henry's son, King Richard I, was more interested in fighting in the Holy Land.

In about 1070 the Turks had captured the Holy Land and had stopped Christian travellers from visiting the holy places where Jesus had lived.

The Pope ordered all Christians to recapture the Holy Land. Knights

a Crusader, from a French manuscript

from all over Europe answered his call, but it was not until 1190 that English knights were led on a *Crusade* by their king, Richard I.

Krak des Chevaliers, one of the powerful castles built by the Crusaders in the Holy Land

In 1191 Richard's army defeated the army of Saladin, Sultan of Egypt, at the battle of Arsouf. But, in spite of this victory, the Crusade failed and Richard was killed fighting in France a few years later

47

The Magna Carta

The Norman barons, who owned lands in England and France, used their great riches to build strong castles. By 1215, a number of the barons had banded together and became so powerful that they forced King John to grant the Magna Carta (Great Charter).

The Great Charter was partly an agreement that the King should not tax the barons unfairly, but it also gave a lot of details about how the kingdom should be ruled justly. In later centuries it was seen as a protection of people's freedom.

Under Henry III, who came to the throne at the age of nine, a group of barons, led by Simon de Montfort, Earl of Leicester, became very powerful. At one point they actually ruled England in place of the king.

Simon de Montfort's shield. He and his wife, Eleanor, sister of the King, owned nearly a quarter of England. De Montfort was killed at the battle of Evesham in 1265.

Simon de Montfort and the Council of Barons called on the help of knights and important citizens to rule England. This was an important step in the development of Parliament.

ROMANS
700BC – AD383

SAXONS
AND
NORMANS
383 – 1272.

MIDDLE
AGES
1272 – 1485

TUDORS
1485 – 1603

1083 yrs   889 yrs   213 yrs   118 yrs

TIMELINE GUIDE TO *A HISTORY OF BRITAIN*

How we know

The events in this book happened over seven hundred years ago – so how do we know about them?

Historians use EVIDENCE, rather like detectives do, to piece a story together.

Some BOOKS describing Saxon, Viking and Norman life have survived to this day. The Vikings wrote many sagas which are full of interesting details of life at the time.

There are also a lot of BUILDINGS which still survive. The Normans built many stone cathedrals and castles. There is a list of places to visit on page 56.

excavation of the Anglo-Saxon burial ship at Sutton Hoo in the 1930s

STUARTS 1603 – 1714	GEORGIANS 1714 – 1830	VICTORIANS 1830 – 1901	MODERN TIMES 1901 – 1945

111 yrs ▸ 116 yrs ▸ 71 yrs ▸ 44 yrs ▸

Archaeologists have *excavated* many sites. One very interesting excavation in York has revealed the Viking town of Jorvik.

OBJECTS found by archaeologists are often stored in museums. Most of the objects are made of metal, pottery or stone. We have fewer objects made from cloth or wood because they rot easily. One marvellous cloth object that has survived is the *Bayeux Tapestry*, which was finished by about 1082. It tells the story of the Norman invasion.

A reconstruction of the magnificent helmet that was found in the Sutton Hoo ship

Some of these old objects seem strange to us. What do you think this is? You will find the answer on page 56

Legacy

The Britain known to the Saxons, Vikings and Normans was very different from the one we know today.

Then, most people could not read or write. Many children did not live to be adults and most people spent all their lives in one village or town. Much of the country was made up of woodlands and forests. Deer, wolves, bears and eagles were common.

The origins of some of our place names tell us this. **Derby** means 'many deer near one village'. **Everton** comes from **eofor**, which meant 'wild boar that lived in forests'.

Did you know?

When we use the words **widow**, **penny**, **hill**, **eggs**, **little** and **morning** we are using Saxon and Viking words.

The Anglo-Saxons and Vikings gave us **Wessex** (now no longer used) which meant 'place of the West Saxons', **Norfolk** (North folk), and **Suffolk** (South folk). Even the word **England** itself comes from 'the country where the Angles live' – Angleland.

Interesting word meanings

word	meaning	example
worth	enclosure, farm	Tamworth (farm on the River Tame)
ham	home, village	Durham
ton	town, village, farm	Brighton
burgh	stronghold	Bamburgh
ing	place of a family	Reading (place of the people of Reada)
ford	river crossing	Stamford (the ford with the stony (Stam) bottom)
chipping	market (to sell is 'cheaping')	Chipping Camden
by	village	Whitby
thorpe	smaller village	Mablethorpe

The Vikings gave us the names of four days of the week:

TUESDAY	named after TIW, the god of battle
WEDNESDAY	named after WODEN, the chief god
THURSDAY	named after THOR, the thunder god
FRIDAY	named after FREY, the goddess of crops

Glossary the following words appear in the text in *italics*

archaeologist: someone who digs up and studies ancient remains

baron: an important Norman noble

Bayeux Tapestry: a long embroidery, not a tapestry, made by English needlewomen after the Battle of Hastings. It is 70 metres long and tells the story of the Norman invasion of England in pictures

burh: (pronounced BUR): a fortified town

Celts: Ancient Britons

chausses: chain mail pantaloons to protect the legs

convert: to change someone's religion

Crusade: a war to recapture the Holy Land. It means a 'war of the cross'. The Crusaders wore crosses on their clothes

Danegeld: money paid to stop the Danes attacking

ealdormen: powerful landowners

excavate: to dig up ancient remains

fee (fief): part of a baron's land

feudalism: an arrangement by which people gave services to their lord in return for his protection

fyrd: the Saxon army, led by King Alfred

mead: a strong alcoholic drink made from honey

motte: a manmade earth mound

pagans: people who worship many different gods

Plantagenet: line of Norman kings after Stephen, who took their name from the 'plante genista', a yellow flower worn as a crest on their helmets

replica: a copy

synod: a meeting of church leaders

tenant: someone who rents property or land

Viking: raiders from Norway, Sweden and Denmark. They were often just called 'Danes'

wergild: the fine for murder. It means 'man price'

Index

Some places you can visit to find out more about the Saxons, the Vikings and the Normans

SAXONS
Bradford-on-Avon (St Lawrence Church), Wiltshire
British Museum, London (Sutton Hoo Treasure)
Deerhurst (St Mary's Church), Gloucestershire
Durham Cathedral Museum, Durham
Greensted (St Andrew's Church), Essex
Gurness Broch, Orkney
Lincoln Museum, Lincoln
Monkwearmouth (St Peter's Church), Tyne and Wear
Offa's Dyke, along the borders of England and Wales
Wareham, Dorset
Weald and Downland Open Air Museum, Sussex
West Stow, Suffolk (reconstructed houses)

VIKINGS
Jorvik Viking Centre, York
Manx Museum, Douglas, Isle of Man
Yorkshire Museum, York

NORMANS
Battle Abbey, East Sussex
British Museum, London (copy of the *Bayeux Tapestry*)
Durham Cathedral, Durham
Ely Cathedral, Ely, Cambridgeshire
Glastonbury Abbey, Somerset
Hedingham Castle, Essex
Iffley (St Mary's Church), Oxfordshire
Lincoln Cathedral, Lincoln
Oakham Castle, Leicestershire
Peterborough Cathedral, Cambridgeshire
Pickering Castle, North Yorkshire
Tower of London

The picture on page 50 shows a Viking board, made out of whalebone, which may have been used for 'ironing'. It was found in Norway where bun-shaped glass objects, which may have been used for smoothing out cloth, have also been found